American Symbols

Our U.S. Capitol

by Mary Firestone

illustrated by Matthew Skeens

PICTURE WINDOW BOOKS
Minneapolis, Minnesota

Special thanks to our advisers for their expertise:

Diane K. Skvarla, Curator
United States Senate

Terry Flaherty, Ph.D., Professor of English
Minnesota State University, Mankato

✦

Editor: Shelly Lyons
Designers: Abbey Fitzgerald, Amy Muehlenhardt, and Tracy Davies
Page Production: Melissa Kes
Art Director: Nathan Gassman
Associate Managing Editor: Christianne Jones
The illustrations in this book were created digitally.
Photo Credit: Photodisc, 23

Picture Window Books
5115 Excelsior Boulevard, Suite 232
Minneapolis, MN 55416
877-845-8392
www.picturewindowbooks.com

Library of Congress Cataloging-in-Publication Data
Firestone, Mary.
Our U.S. Capitol / by Mary Firestone ; illustrated by Matthew Skeens.
p. cm. — (American symbols)
Includes index.
ISBN-13: 978-1-4048-3719-5 (library binding)
ISBN-10: 1-4048-3719-1 (library binding)
1. United States Capitol (Washington, D.C.)—Juvenile literature. 2. Washington (D.C.)—Buildings,
structures, etc.—Juvenile literature. I. Skeens, Matthew. II. Title. III. Title: Our United States Capitol.
F204.C2F57 2008
975.3—dc22   2007004587

208.7
R.1

Table of Contents

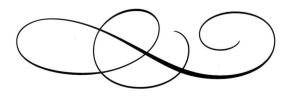

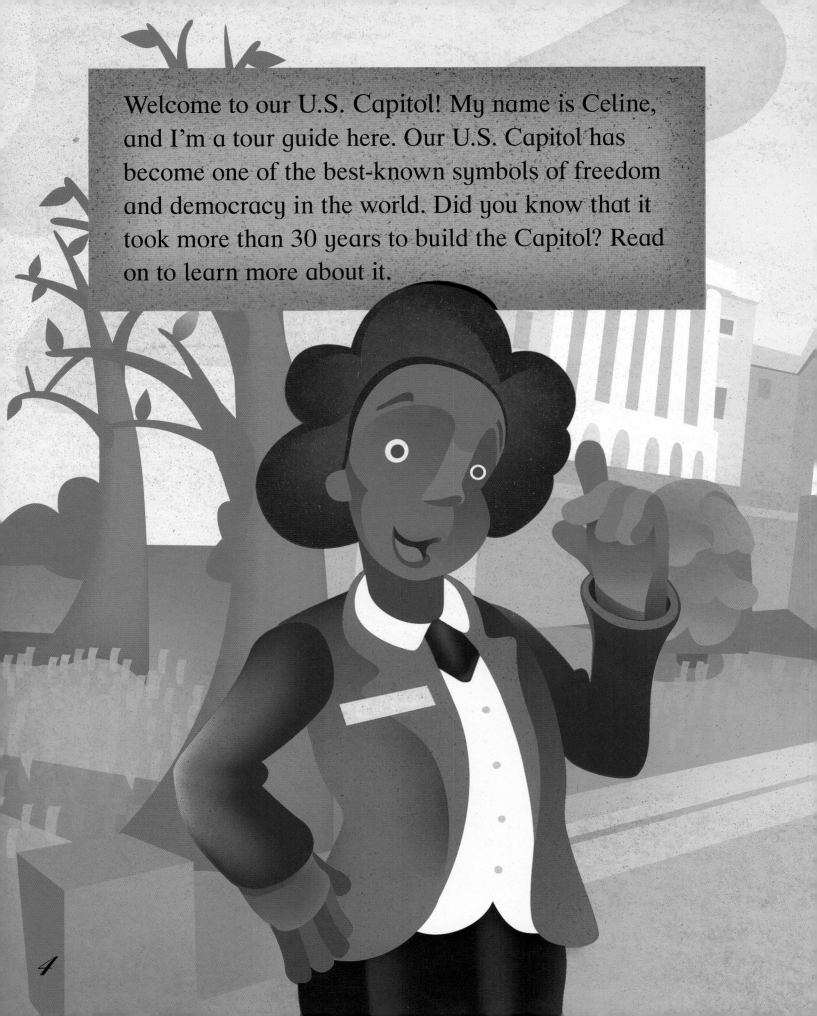

Welcome to our U.S. Capitol! My name is Celine, and I'm a tour guide here. Our U.S. Capitol has become one of the best-known symbols of freedom and democracy in the world. Did you know that it took more than 30 years to build the Capitol? Read on to learn more about it.

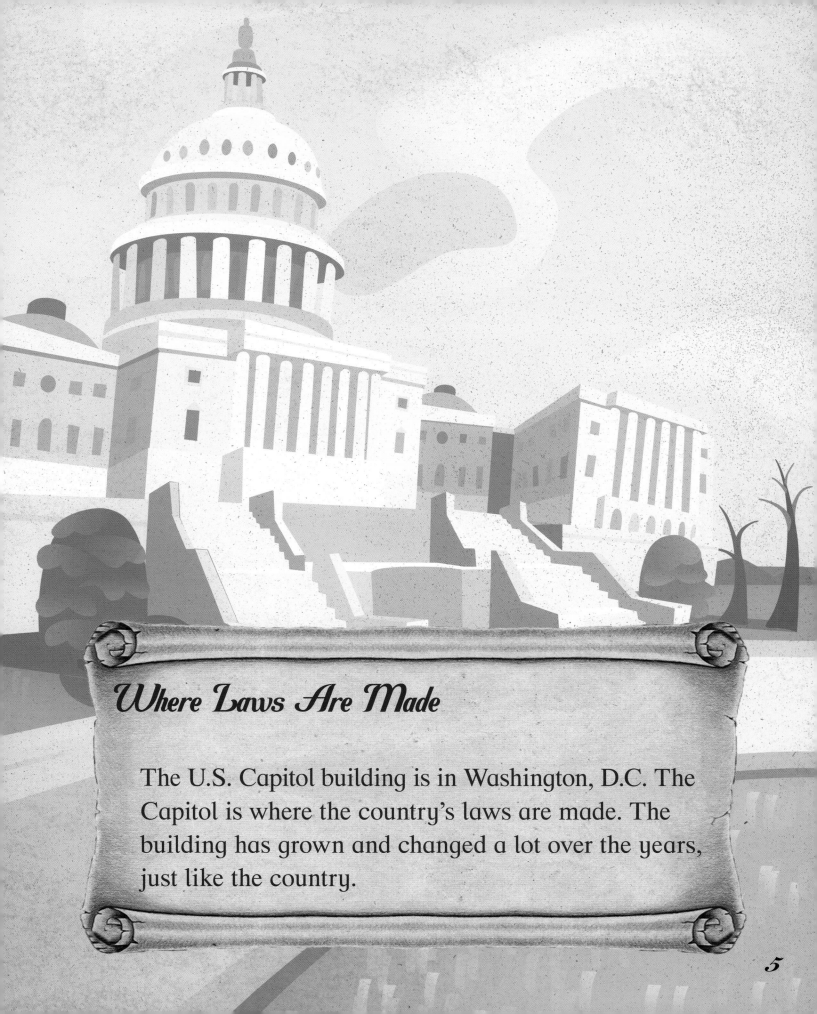

Where Laws Are Made

The U.S. Capitol building is in Washington, D.C. The Capitol is where the country's laws are made. The building has grown and changed a lot over the years, just like the country.

The Location

In 1790, leaders of the United States decided on a capital city and named it Washington, after the country's first president, George Washington.

That same year, the U.S. Congress passed a law that said a Capitol building would be built. It would be located on the banks of the Potomac River.

A Winning Idea

Finding someone to design the Capitol building was not easy. Thomas Jefferson, a top government official, suggested having a design contest. The contest promised $500 to the winner. But Washington and Jefferson didn't like of any of the 17 ideas entered in the contest.

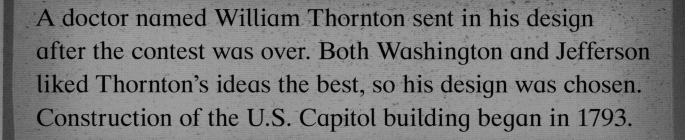

A doctor named William Thornton sent in his design after the contest was over. Both Washington and Jefferson liked Thornton's ideas the best, so his design was chosen. Construction of the U.S. Capitol building began in 1793.

An architect named James Hoban was hired to watch over Thornton's project. Hoban had designed the White House before he worked on the U.S. Capitol.

Parts of the Capitol

Thornton's design had a dome and rotunda in the center and large wings, or sections, to the north and south.

The north wing was finished in 1800. It housed the Senate Chamber. In the same wing, the Supreme Court Chamber was completed in 1810.

The south wing was finished in 1807. The House of Representatives met in the House Chamber in the south wing.

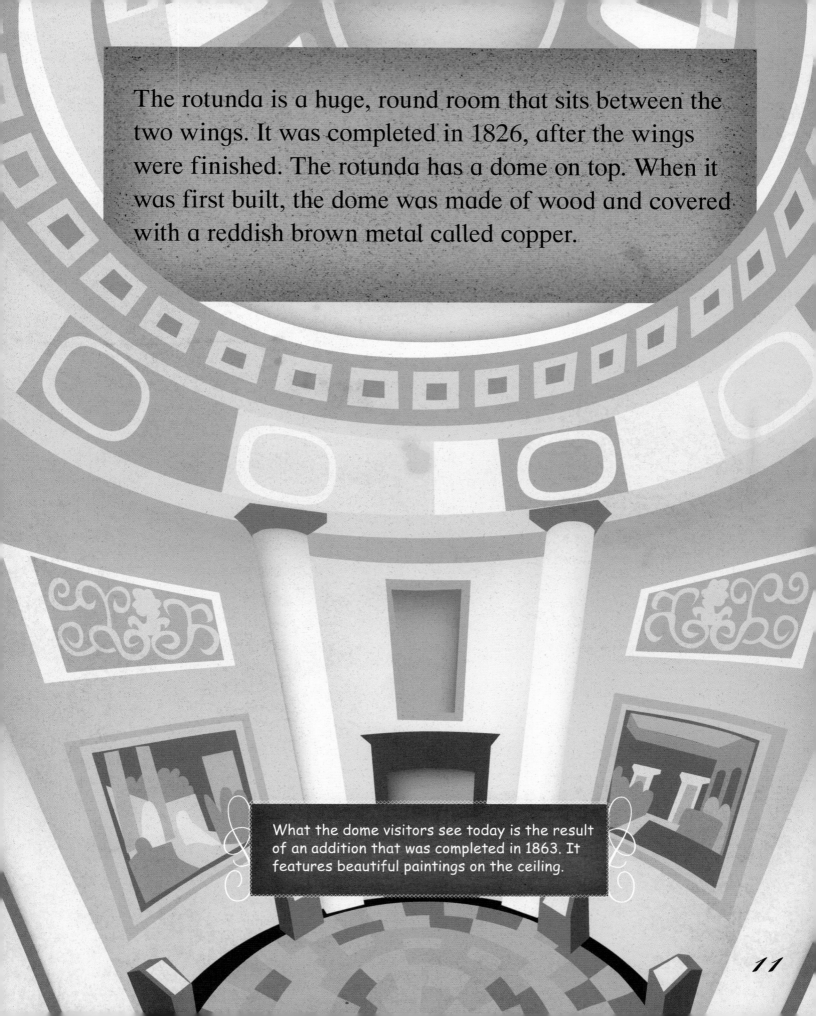

The rotunda is a huge, round room that sits between the two wings. It was completed in 1826, after the wings were finished. The rotunda has a dome on top. When it was first built, the dome was made of wood and covered with a reddish brown metal called copper.

What the dome visitors see today is the result of an addition that was completed in 1863. It features beautiful paintings on the ceiling.

The Capitol During War

The Capitol building was still unfinished when the War of 1812 (1812–1815) broke out. Battles were fought near Washington, and the British set fire to buildings. As the Capitol burned, a rainstorm moved over the city. The rain put out the flames. The Capitol was still standing, but the insides were nearly destroyed.

After surviving the War of 1812 and the fire, the Capitol was finally finished in 1826—33 years after construction had started.

An architect named Benjamin Henry Latrobe had worked on construction of the Capitol. He was given the job of repairing the Capitol after the War of 1812. Later, a man named Charles Bullfinch took over his job and finished the work.

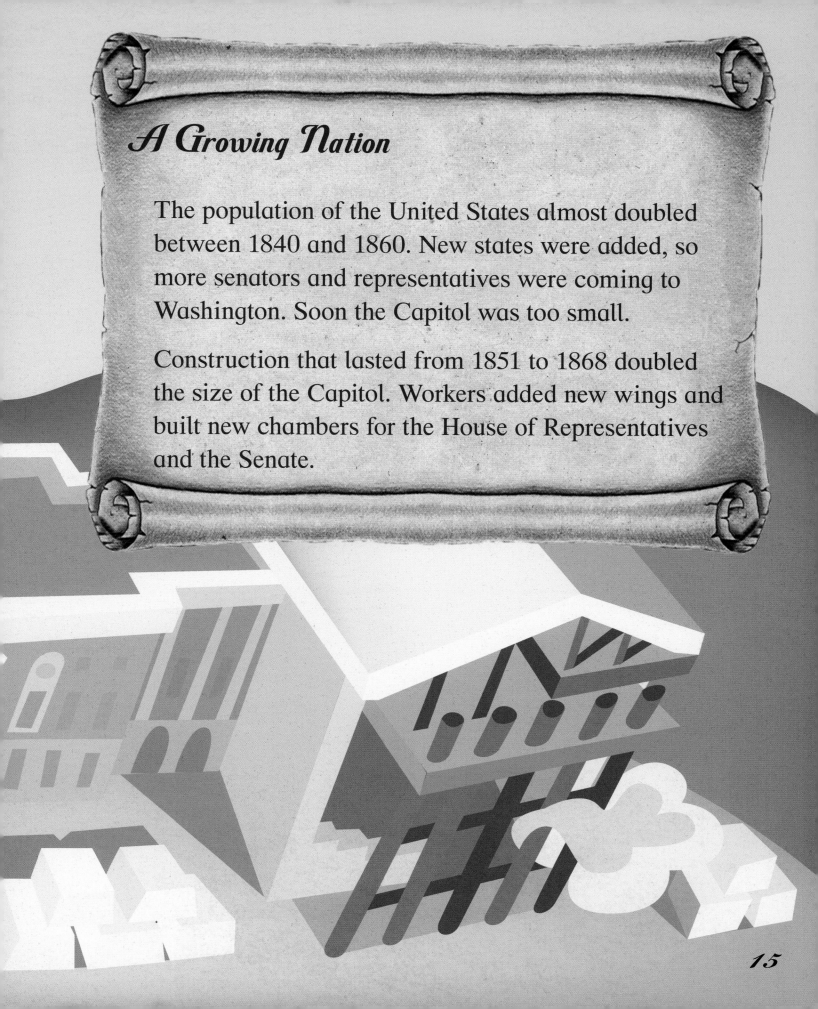

A Growing Nation

The population of the United States almost doubled between 1840 and 1860. New states were added, so more senators and representatives were coming to Washington. Soon the Capitol was too small.

Construction that lasted from 1851 to 1868 doubled the size of the Capitol. Workers added new wings and built new chambers for the House of Representatives and the Senate.

A Bigger Dome

The new wings made the dome at the center of the building look too small. The old dome was removed, and work began on a new one. The new dome was made of cast iron. The metal made it fireproof.

American artist Thomas Crawford created a huge statue called "Freedom" for the top of the dome. It stood more than 19 feet (5.8 m) tall. "Freedom" was placed on top of the dome more than 140 years ago.

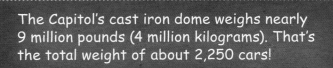

The Capitol's cast iron dome weighs nearly 9 million pounds (4 million kilograms). That's the total weight of about 2,250 cars!

A Soldiers' Hospital

When the Civil War (1861–1865) began, the construction at the Capitol stopped briefly. President Abraham Lincoln thought that if construction continued, it would be a good sign that the country would make it through the war. Soon, Congress ordered the construction on the wings to restart.

During the war, soldiers lived in the Capitol. The building also served as a hospital for wounded troops. The basement was turned into a bakery so soldiers would have a fresh supply of bread.

Throughout the years, the Capitol has changed to keep up with the times. In the 1850s, the building got indoor plumbing. Electricity was added in the 1880s. Air conditioning was added in 1928.

A Modern Capitol

In 1962, a very large addition was finished on the east front side of the Capitol. In 1976, the old Senate chamber, National Statuary Hall, and the old Supreme Court chamber were restored. In 1983, the west walls of the Capitol were strengthened and restored.

Throughout the years, the Capitol has gotten its own power plant, subway system, and post office. In some ways, it works like a small city.

Millions of people visit our U.S. Capitol each year. It is a symbol of freedom and democracy. Visitors can even watch members of Congress in action.

With so many visitors, Congress added the Capitol Visitor Center in 2007 to improve comfort and safety for everyone.

I hope you enjoyed learning about the U.S. Capitol. Come visit soon!

U.S. Capitol Facts

∞ French architect Pierre L'Enfant was the first man hired to design the Capitol. But he was fired in 1792 because he wouldn't make drawings of his designs. He said he had the plans in his head.

∞ The south wing of the U.S. Capitol holds National Statuary Hall, where statues of successful U.S. citizens are on display. They include former leaders, artists, teachers, and religious figures.

∞ The U.S. flag flies over the House and Senate wings of the Capitol when Congress is in session. At night, a lantern on the top of the dome is also lit, to show that Congress is working.

The Capitol

Glossary

architect — a person who plans what new buildings will look like and decides how the rooms will fit together

chamber — a room where government leaders meet

Civil War — (1861–1865) the battle between states in the North and South that led to the end of slavery in the United States

Congress — the group of people in the U.S. government who make laws

democracy — a kind of government in which the people make decisions by voting

dome — a raised, round roof

House of Representatives — one of the two houses of the U.S. Congress; it has 435 members, called representatives

restored — to have brought something back to its original condition

rotunda — a large, round room covered by a dome

Senate — one of the two houses of the U.S. Congress; it has 100 members, called senators; each state has two senators

Supreme Court — the most powerful court in the United States

symbol — an object that stands for something else

War of 1812 — (1812–1815) a war between the United States and Great Britain over unfair British control of shipping; often called the "Second War of Independence"

To Learn More

At the Library

Britton, Tamara L. *The Capitol.* Edina, Minn.: ABDO Publishing Co., 2003.

DeGezelle, Terri. *The U.S. Capitol.* Mankato, Minn.: Capstone Press, 2004.

Hempstead, Anne. *The U.S. Capitol.* Chicago: Heinemann Library, 2006.

On the Web

FactHound offers a safe, fun way to find Web sites related to this book. All of the sites on FactHound have been researched by our staff.

1. Visit *www.facthound.com*
2. Type in this special code: 1404837191
3. Click on the FETCH IT button.

Your trusty FactHound will fetch the best sites for you!

Index

Look for all of the books in the American Symbols series:

The Bald Eagle
The Bill of Rights
The Great Seal of the United States
The Liberty Bell
The Lincoln Memorial
Our American Flag

Our National Anthem
Our U.S. Capitol
The Pledge of Allegiance
The Statue of Liberty
The U.S. Constitution
The White House